RULES OF GOLF

A Handy Fast Guide to Golf Rules 2020 - 2021 (Pocket Sized Edition)

TeamGolfwell

Published by Pacific Trust Holdings NZ Ltd.

This is a quick reference book to the Rules of Golf. The pronouns used in this book use the masculine gender but also include the feminine gender and the singular shall include the plural, and vice versa as the context requires.

HOW THIS BOOK WORKS

This book will answer most every golf rule question in clear understandable language and gives you a quick overview of the rules and penalties which come into play when you need a fast answer. It includes the USGA and R & A 2019 major changes as well as the golf rules that come up often and didn't change and can be used for stroke play and match play.

The rules are in 7 sections for the course area where the rules come into play for easy reference: **Before Starting Play, Tee Area, General Area (Fairway & Rough, etc.), Relief in the General Area, Penalty Areas, Bunkers, and Greens.** Some rules are repeated in several sections for quick reference. Stroke and match play rules are included.

The next several pages, **"QUICK RULES SUMMARY"** will answer most every golf rule question in seconds with more information shown in the page reference along with the official golf rule reference.

You don't have to remember all the rules if you keep this guide handy for fast answers to most every rule question and what to do next. Happy golfing!

Sincerely, Team Golfwell

QUICK RULES SUMMARY

BEFORE STARTING PLAY

PRACTICING ON THE COURSE BEFORE THE ROUND -   Generally not allowed in stroke play but generally allowed in match play.   In match play a player may practice on the course *before* a round or between rounds of a match-play competition subject to Committee regulations (Rule 5).

In stroke play, a player can't generally practice on the course *before* a round but can practice putting or chipping by the first tee. The Committee can adopt a local rule regulating this (Rule 5).

PRACTICING ON THE COURSE DURING A ROUND – Not allowed when playing a hole. A player cannot practice on the course while playing a hole. Between holes, a player can practice putting or chipping on the green just played or the next tee (but not in bunkers) provided it doesn't delay play (Rule 5).

PLAYERS ARE SUPPOSED TO CALL PENALTIES ON THEMSELVES – DQ

(Disqualified) if player knowingly doesn't call a penalty on himself. Players are expected to recognize when they have breached a rule and be honest and apply their own penalties. If a player knows he broke a rule and doesn't apply it the penalty is DQ (Rule 1).

"GENERAL PENALTY" – Means a 2-stroke penalty in stroke play and loss of hole in match play. In stroke play, a breach of a rule may result in these penalties: a 1 stroke penalty, a "general penalty" which is a 2-stroke penalty, or disqualification (Rule 3).

In match play, A "general penalty" is loss of hole (Definitions). Most rules apply to both, but certain rules apply in only one or the other as described herein (Rule 3).

CHECK LOCAL RULES – Check for no play zones, lift clean and place, drop zones, etc. Check the golf course website, notice board, scorecard, etc. for local rules. They will usually help you.

STROKE PLAY – Must hole out and lowest score wins. The lowest score over 18 holes wins and you must hole-out every hole (Rule 3).

MATCH PLAY – Based on holes won. In match play, the player and his opponent compete against each other on each hole. Each individual hole is a contest won by the person who completes the hole with the fewest strokes. If each player has the same score for a hole, the hole is "halved", i.e. a tie (Rule 3). Score cards aren't required in match play.

A player wins the match when he has won more holes than what is left to play. For example, if you are three holes up with only two holes left to play, you win "three to two." If you are tied at the end (all square), the match is "halved."

Stroke play requires holing out each hole. In match play, you may concede a putt (or any stroke) by telling your opponent to "pick up." You can also concede a golf hole and/or an entire match. Once you make a concession you are not allowed to withdraw it (Rule 3).

MAXIMUM SCORE FORMAT – Allows player to pick up after reaching the max score for that hole. Effective 2019, there is a new official form of stroke play called "Maximum Score" which allows players to pick up on a hole once the player reaches the maximum score for a hole (it helps the pace of play). For example, the golf course Committee can set the maximum score at net double bogey, or two times par, or whatever they decide for each hole (Rule 21). You normally must hole out on every hole in stroke play but not when you are playing maximum score (see Rule 3).

BE ON TIME FOR YOUR TEE TIME TO AVOID PENALTIES – Less than 5 minutes late is a general penalty and more than 5 minutes late may be DQ (Disqualified).   If you are less than 5 minutes late for your tee time, you incur a general penalty on the first hole. If you are more than 5 minutes late, you can be disqualified. The Committee may excuse you under exceptional circumstances (Rule 5).

SLOW PLAY – 1 stroke for first delay, general penalty for second delay and DQ for third delay. Effective 2019, players are encouraged not to linger and keep their pace of play consistent. Players are encouraged to play their shot within 40 seconds once they become able to do so and there are no other distractions. A golf course Committee can adopt a pace of play policy with certain requirements. The penalty for unreasonably delaying play while on a hole or between holes was revised in 2019 to a 1 stroke penalty for the first breach, a general penalty for the second breach, and DQ for the third breach. If the unreasonable delay occurs between holes the penalty is applied to the next hole (Rule 5.6).

DISTANCE MEASURING DEVICES - Allowed. Effective 2019, Distance Measuring Devices (DMDs) are allowed unless the golf club Committee prohibits their use (Rule 4).

CODE OF CONDUCT – Possible penalties.
Getting overly angry, or outrageous conduct
may violate the golf course code of conduct
established by the golf course Committee.
Effective 2019, a Committee can adopt a code
of conduct and penalize a player for violating
the course's code of conduct during play (Rule
1).

**14 CLUBS MAX – If more than 14, the
penalty is 2 strokes per hole (4 holes max)
or loss of hole (2 holes max).** In stroke play,
once a player becomes aware his clubs exceed
14 there is a 2-stroke penalty for each hole
played in breach of this rule with a maximum
penalty of 4 strokes in the round (Rule 4).

In match play, once a player becomes aware of
it, he loses 1 hole for each hole played with
more than 14 clubs with a maximum deduction
of 2 holes in the round (Rule 4).

If you discover you have more than 14 clubs
before beginning play, announce it, and leave

the extra club(s) behind or turned upside down in your bag without penalty (Rule 4).

LOSE A CLUB DURING PLAY – Player must play without it. If you lose a club during play that's later found, you may use it again. But if it can't be found, you must play without it and you can't add a club (Rule 4).

ADJUSTABLE CLUBS – A player isn't allowed to adjust an adjustable club during play. If you have adjustable clubs, check the adjustments you have made since you are not allowed to adjust them during the round (Rule 4).

TIGHTENING CLUBHEAD OR SHAFT - Allowed. Check for any looseness before you start. If your clubhead or shaft become loose during play, you can tighten them without penalty (Rule 4).

BORROWING OR SHARING OF CLUBS – Not allowed. If a player damages a club when teeing off or during play, he cannot borrow a club or share a club with another player (Rule 4). But playing partners can share clubs so long as they have no more than 14 clubs between them (Rules 22 and 23). You can borrow golf balls (Rule 4).

CHANGING GOLF BALLS – Allowed between holes, when taking relief, or when ball is damaged. You play the same ball from tee to holing-out on a hole. You may change balls without penalty between holes or when taking relief (Rules 6 and 14).

If your ball becomes cut or cracked, you can change balls (Rule 4). Mark it before you lift it to inspect for damage. You cannot clean your ball when inspecting it for damage. If you clean it, you incur a 1 penalty stroke (Rule 14).

MULLIGANS, ETC. – Players can't agree to ignore rules. If two or more players deliberately agree to ignore any rule (e.g., "Let's have one mulligan a side" or "Let's roll 'em in the fairway") they are subject to disqualification when they start the round even if they haven't yet acted on the agreement (Rule 1).

"CLUB LENGTH" Means the longest club in your bag except your putter. The term "club length" means the longest club in your bag except for your putter (Definitions).

TEE AREA

ORDER FOR TEEING OFF ON THE FIRST TEE - Tee off in the order shown on the tee schedule, otherwise, by agreement or random method. After the first hole, play the honors which means the player who scored lowest in stroke play or who won the hole in match play tees off first on the second hole (Rule 6). In four-ball, partners can play in the order they choose (Rule 23).

ADVICE ON THE COURSE – Asking for or giving advice is OK if it's public information (e.g., distances). You can discuss distances to bunkers, penalty areas, etc. or ask about the line of play since it's public information (e.g., "Is this a dogleg right or left?"). There is no penalty for a player giving unsolicited advice (e.g., "I should have used a 6 iron, etc.").

Otherwise, a player can't ask about club selection or tell another player what club to use or how to play a shot, etc. A player who gives or asks for such advice incurs a general penalty (Rule 10).

For a ball on the putting green, you aren't allowed to ask for advice on the line of play (Rule 10). However, partners playing on a side can give advice to each other without penalty to each other (Rule 24).

TEE AREA DIMENSIONS - A rectangular area measuring 2-club lengths back from front edge of tee markers. Tee the ball anywhere in a rectangular area within 2 club lengths from the front edge of the tee markers (Definitions). If you tee off outside this area or hit from the wrong tee markers (assuming those markers are outside of the tee area), you incur a 2-stroke penalty in stroke play and must replay the shot from the correct tee area (Rule 6). In match play, your opponent may elect to cancel your stroke played outside the tee area and have you replay it without penalty (Rule 6).

Taking your stance outside the tee area is allowed if your ball is inside the tee area (Rule 6).

USING A TEE – A player is not required to use a tee when teeing off. You may play your ball from the ground in the tee area. You can improve certain conditions in the tee area by altering the surface. For example, you can make an indentation using your club, press down the soil, bend or break grass, etc. (Rule 6 and 8.1b (8)).

USING TWIGS, ETC. TO LINE UP A SHOT – Not allowed. You can't place a twig, part of a leaf, etc. to help you line up your tee shot or any shot or you incur a general penalty (Rule 8).

WHIFFS – They count as strokes. If you intentionally attempt to hit a golf ball and miss it entirely, it counts as a stroke and the ball is in play. If your ball is still in the tee area, you may re-tee it (Rule 6).

IF A PLAYER ACCIDENTALLY HITS THE BALL OR IF IT FALLS OFF THE TEE BY ITSELF – There is no penalty and the player may re-tee the ball. If your ball falls off the tee, you can replace it without penalty. If you accidentally knock it off the tee or accidentally knock it away taking a practice swing, it isn't a stroke since the ball is not yet in play. You can re-tee the ball in the tee area (Rule 6).

Once the ball is in play, and you accidentally move your ball you must take a 1 stroke penalty and replace the ball to its original position (Rule 9).

By the way, when you are on the green, if you accidentally move your ball (or ball marker) there is no penalty and you must replace it to where it was before you accidentally moved it (Rule 13).

MOVING TEE MARKERS IS NOT ALLOWED WHEN TEEING OFF – But OK if the player is not on the tee area of the hole being played. When teeing off, you can't move or adjust the tee markers for the hole you are playing (Rule 6). If you hit an errant shot that lands on another tee area, you can move the tee marker without penalty if it's a moveable obstruction. If it is immovable take a 1 club-length drop at the nearest point of relief no nearer the hole (Rule 16).

TEE SHOT GOES OB OR LOST – Play a provisional ball or consider local rule options. When a player hits his ball out of bounds or has a lost ball, there is a 1 stroke penalty and the player must replay the ball from where it was hit (i.e. take stroke and distance relief). A ball is deemed lost if it is not found in 3 minutes once you begin searching for it. If you think you hit your ball OB, or it may be lost, you normally play a provisional ball. You need to announce and say you are playing a "provisional" ball otherwise it becomes a new ball in play under penalty of stroke and distance (Rule 18).

If you can't find your original tee shot ball within 3 minutes or if it's OB, you count the stroke made with your tee shot and the strokes made with the provisional ball and add a penalty stroke and play out the hole with the provisional ball.

Effective 2019, under a new Local Rule, a golf course Committee can elect to give a player an option for dropping a ball without having to go back to the point where you hit the ball that became lost or went OB and when you haven't played a provisional ball.

The Committee has the option to adopt a local rule allowing you to drop another ball and take a 2-stroke penalty to speed up play. This local rule helps a player (and pace of play) who hasn't played a provisional ball from going back to the location of the previous stroke. Under this option, you drop your ball in a large relief area which is between two lines.

The first line is established using the "ball reference point" which is a line drawn from the hole to the ball reference point which is the point where the ball was lost or went out of bounds.

The second line is a line drawn from the hole to the "fairway reference point" and the fairway reference point is a point you mark on the nearest edge of the fairway no nearer the hole.

The relief area is between those two lines. Or, in other words, in the area between where the ball was lost or went out of bounds and the nearest edge of the fairway (no nearer the hole).

Also, this relief area is extended by two club-lengths on the outside edges of the "ball reference point" and the "fairway reference point" (no nearer the hole).

This local rule is not intended for professional play or high amateur competitions but intended to help speed up the pace of play.

The player is not allowed to use this option when his ball is known to be in a penalty area.

If the player's ball is in a penalty area, the player must take penalty area relief. See the Penalty Area Section of this book if your ball went into a penalty area on page 51.

The player is also not allowed to use this option when he has played a provisional ball.

The new rules refer to a Model Local Rule for a golf course Committee to adopt which can be found here > USGA, Draft of Model Local Rule, see this link, "Stroke and Distance: Download the draft text as a PDF", and the link is > http://www.usga.org/content/usga/home-page/ruleshub/rules-modernization/infographics/golf-s-new-rules-stroke-and-distance.html#expanded

IS A BALL OB OR NOT OB? – The entire ball must be out of bounds for it to be OB. For a ball to be out of bounds, the entire ball must be in the OB area and past the front edge of the OB markers. You may take your stance in the OB area to play a ball that isn't OB (Rule 18.2a (2)).

NO PROVISIONAL BALL IS ALLOWED – For a ball hit into a Penalty Area. You cannot play a provisional ball if you are certain your ball is in a penalty area. Penalty areas have their own rules (see p. 30 of this book). You can hit a provisional if you are not certain. For example, if you clearly see your ball splash in a lake (water hazards are now designated as penalty areas) you cannot play a provisional ball and must take penalty area relief. But if you are not certain (e.g., you think your ball might be OB or lost and not in the penalty area) you may play a provisional ball (Rule 18).

BALL ACCIDENTALLY HITS PLAYER OR SOMETHING ELSE – No penalty and play it as it lies. Effective 2019, there is no penalty if you accidentally hit yourself, an opponent, your equipment, another person, animal, object, etc. and you play your next shot as it lies (Rule 11).

REPLACING DAMAGED CLUBS – You can replace a damaged club if you didn't damage it. If you break your driver or another club, you can only replace it if the damage occurred from an "outside influence" or "natural forces" (i.e., a player can replace a club if someone other than the player or his or her caddy damaged the club). For example, if another golf cart runs over your club, you can replace a damaged club if you didn't damage it (Rule 4). It may be impractical to timely run back and get a loaner from the pro shop since you can't unreasonably delay play. The penalty for unreasonably delaying play is one stroke for the first breach, a general penalty for the second breach, and DQ for the third breach (Rule 5).

REPAIRING AND USING A DAMAGED CLUB – Allowed. Effective 2019, a player can use a damaged club even if the player damaged it in anger. A player is also allowed to repair a damaged club and continue to use it (Rule 4).

BALL BREAKS INTO PIECES AFTER A SHOT – Replay the shot without penalty. If you hit your ball and it breaks into pieces after a shot, the shot doesn't count, and the player must replay the shot (Rule 4).

THE GENERAL AREA - FAIRWAY, ROUGH, ETC.

"GENERAL AREA" Means the Fairway, Rough, Fringe, etc. The "general area" of a golf course is everything on the golf course except the following: 1) the teeing area when starting a hole, 2) penalty areas, 3) bunkers, and 4) the putting green for the hole being played (Rule 2 and Definitions).

GOLF COURSE AREAS – A ball is always treated as being in only one area. Different rules apply depending on what area of the course your ball is lying in (Rule 2). You need to determine if your ball is in the general area or a specific area. Specific areas are: 1) the tee area for the hole being played, 2) penalty areas, 3) bunkers, and 4) the putting green for the hole being played.

If your ball is in the general area but also encroaches into a specific area, it is treated as being in the specific area and specific area rules apply. For example, a ball lying part in a penalty area and part in the general area would be treated as being in the penalty area and penalty area rules would apply (Rule 2).

Although it may seldom occur, if a ball comes to rest being part in two specific areas, it is treated as lying in the specific area that comes first in this order: 1. penalty area, 2. bunker, 3. putting green. For example, a ball lying part in a penalty area and part in a bunker would be treated as being in the penalty area and penalty area rules apply (Rules 2 and 17).

ACCIDENTALLY MOVING YOUR BALL IN THEGENERAL AREA – A player incurs 1 penalty stroke if the player causes his ball to move. If a player causes his ball to move (e.g., accidentally hits it when taking a practice swing), he incurs 1 stroke penalty and must replace the ball to where it was before it moved (Rule 9).

ANOTHER BALL INTERFERES WITH YOUR SHOT – Request the other player to mark his ball. If a player reasonably believes that another player's ball might interfere with the player's own play, the player may require the other player to mark the spot and lift the ball. The other player should mark his ball and lift it (but cannot clean it) then the other ball should be played. After the ball is played, the other player replaces his ball in the same lie (recreates it) as best as possible (Rule 15). In stroke play, the other player has an option to play his ball first instead of marking and lifting it (Rule 15.3b(2)).

CLEANING YOUR BALL – Generally allowed when you lift it under the rules except, 1. When you lift it to identify it, 2. When you inspect it for damage, 3. When you lift it since it interferes with another ball, or 4. When you lift it to see if it lies in a condition for relief. When you lift your ball under the rules from the general area (e.g., you encounter temporary water, etc.), you can clean your ball. But you can't clean your ball when you lift it to: 1) to see if the ball is cut or cracked, 2) to identify it, 3) to remove it from interference with the play of another player, or

4) to see if it lies in a condition where relief is allowed.

If you are lifting the ball to identify it, you can only clean the ball to the extent necessary to identify it (Rule 14 and Rule 7).

There is no requirement to announce you are going to lift your ball. Previously, a player had to announce to the other player he was going to lift his ball to identify it. Effective 2019, that is no longer required. This helps the pace of play especially if the other player is across the fairway from you. You may want to announce it anyway to avoid confusion.

LIFTING YOUR BALL ON THE GREEN – You can lift and clean your ball without penalty. Rule 14 allows you to always clean your ball when you lift if from the green.

IMPROVING CONDITIONS OF YOUR SHOT – Not Allowed. Play the ball as it lies. You incur a general penalty if you break off branches, chop off long grass or weeds with practice swings, or do anything which would improve the conditions for your shot (Rule 8). If your ball is extremely difficult to play (e.g., the ball is deep in a heavy bush, etc.) and there is no free relief available under the rules, consider declaring the ball unplayable.

DECLARING A BALL UNPLAYABLE – Gives you 3 Options with 1 penalty stroke: 1. Replay the shot (i.e. stroke and distance), 2. Back-on-the-line Relief or 3. Take a 2-club length lateral drop. If you decide your ball is unplayable you take a 1 stroke penalty and you have 3 options: 1) Go back and replay the shot, 2) Take back-on-the-line relief, i. e., go back on the line to a more favorable spot and drop one club-length on either side of the line no nearer the hole, or 3) Stay where you are and drop within two club-lengths no nearer the hole from your ball's present location (Rule 19).

BALL IS MOVED BY ANOTHER – Replace it without penalty. If your ball comes to rest and is moved by another person, an animal, another ball, etc. you must replace it without penalty. In match play, if your opponent accidentally moves your ball during a search for it, there is no penalty. If it wasn't accidental, your opponent incurs 1 penalty stroke for deliberately moving your ball and you must replace your ball (Rule 9).

BALL MOVED BY NATURAL FORCES – Play it as it lies. If your ball comes to rest in the general area and is blown to another location by the wind or rolls down a hill by itself, you must play the ball from the spot where it came to rest. By the way, if you marked and lifted your ball on the green and *after* replacing your ball it moves, you must replace it to where it was without penalty (Rule 9).

PLACING CLUBS ETC. ON THE GROUND FOR ALIGNMENT – Not allowed. Previously, a player could lay a club down on the ground and use the shaft of the club to help align a shot. Effective 2019, that is no longer allowed anywhere on the course. If you lay a club down or any object on the ground to help your alignment and then take your stance, you incur a general penalty. Caddies are not allowed to stand behind in the line of play.

You cannot avoid the general penalty by your (or the caddy) backing away and removing the club or object after taking your stance (Rule 10).

NOT SURE OF A RULE – Play 2 balls. In stroke play, if you are unsure if you breached a rule or not, you can announce you will play two balls and designate the ball which will count in case there was no breach of the rules. Keep track of the score with each ball until you've holed out for that hole. Then get a ruling from the Committee and then sign your card (Rule 20).

In match play, if you believe your opponent broke a rule and he doesn't agree, you must tell your opponent you're going to request a ruling and then ask a referee once you find a referee or the Committee (Rule 20).

REMOVING LOOSE IMPEDIMENTS – Player incurs 1 penalty stroke if player moves his ball while doing so. You are free to remove loose impediments but if you move your ball while doing so you incur 1 penalty stroke (Rule 15).

Sand and loose soil are not considered to be loose impediments in the general area, but spider webs are loose impediments and can be removed (Definitions).

REMOVING MOVEABLE OBSTRUCTIONS – OK without penalty. A player can remove moveable obstructions without penalty. If your ball moves while removing a moveable obstruction (e.g., a rake) there is no penalty. You must replace your ball to where it was to your best estimate (Rule 15).

LOST BALL – 3-minute search time limit and if not found in 3 minutes it is deemed a lost ball. Previously, you were allowed 5 minutes to search for your ball. Effective 2019, the search time is reduced to 3 minutes.

Check the time when you begin searching. Once 3 minutes have passed it is a lost ball and even if you find your ball just after 3 minutes of searching, you cannot play it since lost ball rules apply (Rule 18).

SEARCHING FOR A BALL AND BALL MOVED DURING SEARCH – Replace it without penalty. Previously, you were penalized if you moved your ball while searching for it. Effective 2019, there is no penalty if you or another person moved it accidentally while searching for your ball. You simply must replace the ball without penalty.

If you don't know the exact spot the ball was at before it was moved, you can estimate the spot to the best of your ability and replace it. This includes recreating the position of your ball on, under or against anything it was on and as close to the spot as you can best estimate (Rule 7).

BALL DEFLECTED ACCIDENTALLY – Play it as it lies without penalty. Generally, if your ball is accidentally deflected by any person or object in the general area, there is no penalty. You play your next shot from where the ball lies (Rule 11). Balls on the greens have different rules for accidental deflections. See the green section on page 40.

PLAYING THE WRONG BALL – A general penalty is incurred. In stroke play, you incur a 2-stroke penalty if you play the wrong ball. After taking the 2-stroke penalty, you locate and play your own ball (Rule 6). If your own ball is lost, you treat it as a lost ball and take stroke and distance relief and go back to where you hit it.

The stroke made with the wrong ball (and any more strokes) does not count. If you don't correct the mistake before teeing off on the next hole you are DQd. If you hit a wrong ball on the final hole, you need to go back and correct it before turning in your scorecard or be DQd (Rule 6).

In match play, the penalty for playing the wrong ball is a general penalty (loss of hole). If the players hit each other's ball, the first to make a stroke at a wrong ball gets loss of hole. If it is not known which wrong ball was played first, there is no penalty and the hole must be played out with the balls exchanged (Rule 6).

SOMEONE PLAYS YOUR BALL – Replace your ball or another ball to where it was and continue play. Replace your ball or substitute another ball on the spot where your ball was mistakenly played by another. If the exact spot isn't known you estimate where it was to the best of your ability (Rule 6 and 14).

DOUBLE OR MULTIPLE HIT BALL – Counts as 1 stroke. Effective 2019, there is no penalty for an accidental double hit or accidental multiple hits in one stroke and they only count as one stroke. The player must play the next ball as it lies (Rule 10).

READY GOLF - Allowed. Normally, the player who is furthest from the hole plays first. If you play out of turn, your opponent in match play has the option of cancelling your shot and have you replay it. There is no penalty in stroke play unless two or more players agree to play out of order to give one of them an advantage and if they do this, then those players each incur a general penalty (Rule 6).

Effective 2019, players can agree amongst themselves to play "ready golf" and allow players in their group who are ready to take their shot to do so (Rule 6).

ADVICE (ASKING FOR OR GIVING ADVICE) – Only allowed if it's public information. You can discuss distances to the green, bunkers, penalty areas, or the line of play or any matter that is public information. Otherwise, you can't give or ask for advice from another player (e.g. "What club did you use?" etc.) or incur a general penalty (Rule 10).

You are also not allowed to ask for advice on the line of play on the putting green for the hole being played (Rule 10).

Partners playing on a side can give advice without penalty to each other (Rule 24).

LIGHTNING – Mark and pick up. You are not required to keep playing if you reasonably believe there is danger from lightning. Mark your ball and resume play when it's clear of lightning (Rule 5).

RELIEF IN THE GENERAL AREA

MARK THE BALL BEFORE LIFTING – If not marked, the player incurs 1 penalty stroke. Place a marker, coin, etc. right behind or right next to the ball or hold a club on the ground right behind or next to the ball before lifting it or incur 1 penalty stroke (Rule 14).

CHANGING GOLF BALLS – Is allowed when taking relief, between holes, or if your ball is damaged. Effective 2019, you can substitute another ball between holes or when you take relief (Rules 6 and 14). If your ball becomes cut or cracked, you can substitute another ball (Rule 4). Mark it before you lift it to inspect for damage. You are not allowed to clean your ball when inspecting it for damage under penalty of 1 stroke. You replace your ball (or another ball if your ball is cut or cracked) on the spot you marked (Rule 14).

FINDING NEAREST POINT OF RELIEF – No nearer the hole. You need to locate the nearest point of relief when you take free relief from an abnormal course condition, a dangerous animal condition, a wrong green or a no play zone. For example, if your ball comes to rest on an immovable obstruction like a concrete cart path, you can play the ball as it lies, or you may want to take free relief and if so, the rules require you to find the nearest point of relief.

To find the nearest point of relief, you look around (i.e., to the right, left and behind you) for a spot off the cart path (no nearer the hole).

You decide what club you reasonably would have used to make the shot from the point your ball came to rest on the cart path. Let's say you decide you would have used an 8iron for your next shot. With your 8-iron, take your stance on the nearest point of relief which may be to the right, left or behind you. When you take your stance, first determine if there is complete relief (for example, let's say when you move to the right there is a still a section of the cart path which interferes with your stance or swing). So, you check other spots to the left and behind you and say you find a spot to the left which is nearest to the ball on the cart path and there is no interference at all from the cart path or anything else. This is the nearest point of relief and you mark it with a tee or other marker.

Then you measure a club length with the longest club in your bag (except your putter) to the sides and behind this point - no closer to the hole - and this is the relief area where you can take a drop.

Again, keep in mind if you aren't happy with dropping in the relief area, you can still play your ball as it lies on the cart path. But, if you are happy with it, lift your ball off the path and drop it in the relief area and play your next shot (Definitions and Rule 16).

ABNORMAL GROUND CONDITIONS – You get free relief for animal holes, G.U.R., Immovable obstructions, or temporary water. Abnormal course conditions are 1) an animal hole, 2) G.U.R (ground under repair), 3) immovable obstructions (e.g., a concrete cart path, sprinkler head, etc.), or 4) temporary water (Rule 16).

If your ball comes to rest in or on an abnormal ground condition in the general area, or if the condition interferes with your stance or swing, you may either play your ball as it lies or take free relief.

If you are certain your ball went into an abnormal course condition area, but you cannot find your ball within 3 minutes (e.g., rolled into an overgrown G.U.R. area, etc.), you get free relief. To take free relief, find the nearest point of relief no nearer the hole where the condition doesn't interfere with your stroke, stance or swing and drop your ball or another ball within one club-length (Rule 16).

ANIMAL HOLES – Free relief. Previously, you were only given free relief from "burrowing animal" holes. Effective 2019, you can take relief from all holes dug by animals regardless if it was a burrowing animal or not. There is no free relief however from holes made by worms, insects and similar invertebrates (Rule 16).

TEMPORARY WATER – Free relief.   Puddles on the course in the general area are temporary water. It isn't enough for the ground to be merely wet, muddy or soft, or for the water to be momentarily visible as the player steps on the area. For a puddle to be temporary water, the accumulation of water must remain present either before or after you take your stance. Dew and frost are not temporary water. You can play your ball as it lies if you wish to, or you can take free relief to the nearest point of relief and drop your ball within 1 club-length no nearer the hole (Rule 16).

DANGEROUS ANIMAL CONDITIONS – Free relief.   You can take free relief to the nearest point of relief if you encounter a dangerous animal condition (Rule 16). If there is a dangerous animal condition which interferes with your stroke (e.g. poisonous snakes, wasp nests, alligators, fire ants, etc.), you can take free relief by finding the nearest point of relief. The nearest point of relief is where the dangerous animal condition no longer exists no nearer the hole and take a 1 club-length drop from that point (Rule 16).

MOVEABLE OBSTRUCTIONS – Free relief. You can remove moveable obstructions without penalty (e.g., ropes, a tee marker on the tee area for another hole, stakes, small and large debris, etc.). If your ball moves, you replace your ball to where it was without penalty (Rule 15).

BALL COMES TO REST UPON A MOVEABLE OBSTRUCTION – Free relief. If your ball comes to rest upon a moveable obstruction (e.g., a collapsed umbrella, a towel, paper bag, etc.), drop your ball within 1 club-length in the same area from where the ball was no nearer the hole (Rule 15).

EMBEDDED BALL – Free relief. Previously, you could only remove an embedded ball if it was embedded in the fairway. Effective 2019, you can play the ball as it lies or take a free drop if your ball is embedded in the general area, i.e., the rough, semi-rough, the fairway, etc. Mark the spot behind the ball and lift it, clean it and take a free drop from knee height within one club-length from your mark no nearer the hole (Rule 16).

INCORRECT GREEN – Free relief. Previously, if your ball came to rest on the wrong green you had to pick it up and play your ball on the nearest point of relief off the green no closer to the hole. You could take your stance on the green itself to play your next shot.

Effective 2019, you are no longer allowed to take your stance on the green or to take a stance where the path of your swing might encounter the surface of the green. You must drop your ball so you won't be taking a stance on the green and the path of your swing will not be able to contact the surface of the green (Rule 13).

**DROPPING FROM KNEE HEIGHT –
Procedures, etc.** Prior to 2019, you had to
hold the ball at shoulder height and drop it.
Now you must drop the ball from knee height
(Rule 14.3). A player might accidentally (or out
of old habit) drop from shoulder height. If this
happens, the player must pick up his ball
before playing it and drop it again from knee
height without penalty.

If the player doesn't drop it from knee height or
doesn't drop it in the relief area but the ball
comes to rest in the proper relief area, he
incurs 1 penalty stroke if he plays the stroke
(Rule 14).

If he drops it properly from knee height and the
ball rolls out of the relief area, he incurs a
general penalty if he plays it.

When the player drops the ball from knee
height, the ball cannot touch any part of the
player's body or equipment on the way down
before it hits the ground. Otherwise, the player
must drop it again without penalty.

A ball must be dropped in a relief area and come to rest in that relief area. If it rolls out, drop it again and if it rolls out a second time, place the ball where it hit the ground in the relief area on the spot where the ball hit the ground on the second drop.

If you drop from knee height and the ball hits the ground and accidentally hits a person or object after hitting the ground and comes to rest in the relief area, that is a legal drop and you cannot elect to re-drop it and you must play the ball as it lies in the relief area (Rule 14).

BALL ROLLS OUT OF RELIEF AREA AFTER DROP - Procedures. As pointed out in the prior section, when you drop a ball, your ball must land in, come to rest and be played from the relief area. If it doesn't come to rest in the relief area, the player is to drop it again a second time, and if it again doesn't come to rest in the relief area, the player is to place the ball on the spot where he dropped it a second time.

Let's say, the player places his ball on the spot where his second drop hit the ground and it still doesn't come to rest but rolls away. In that case, if a dropped ball fails to stay in the relief area after two drops, and then fails to remain on the spot when placed, it must be placed on the same spot again and if it rolls away again, the player must place a ball on the nearest spot where the ball will stay at rest (Rule 14).

DROPPING WHEN A PLAYER SHOULD HAVE REPLACED OR VICE-VERSA – Player incurs a general penalty. If you mistakenly drop your ball instead of replacing it when the rules require you to replace it, or vice-versa, you incur a general penalty if you play the shot. If you realize the mistake before playing the shot and follow the correct procedure (i.e., you drop the ball then realize you had to replace it and before playing the shot you replace it correctly) there is no penalty (Rule 14).

ANOTHER BALL INTERFERES WITH YOUR PLAY – Ask the other player to mark it or the other player can play his ball first in

stroke play. If another ball is too close to your ball so that it interferes with your shot, there are 2 options. First, you can ask the other player to lift it. The other player then marks and lifts his ball. If the other player fails to mark it or cleans his ball, he incurs a 1 stroke penalty. Second, in stroke play, the other player has the option to play first rather than mark and lift his ball (Rule 15).

EMBEDDED BALL IN SAND FILLED FAIRWAY DIVOT OR DRAIN – Possible free relief in the general area if grass is cut to fairway height. This may be a gray area, but if a ball is truly embedded in sand on the fairway or another part of the general area, an argument can be made that free relief is allowed if the sand in which your ball is embedded is in the general area that is cut to fairway height or less. This would mean in effect, you get relief for a ball embedded in its own pitch mark in a sand-filled divot or drain on the fairway provided the sand or drain is in an area cut to fairway height or less (Rule 16.3a and exceptions under that rule).

PENALTY FOR OB OR LOST BALL – Stroke and distance or follow local rules. When a player hits his ball from the general area out of bounds or his ball is lost, he incurs a 1 stroke penalty and the player must go back and play the ball from the original place where it was (i.e., take a stroke and distance relief). A ball is deemed lost if it is not found in 3 minutes once you begin searching for it. If you think you hit your ball OB, or it may be lost, you normally play a provisional ball from where you hit your original ball.

You play your provisional ball up to where you estimate your original ball went. If you can't find your ball or if it's OB, you count the stroke of the first ball and the strokes of the provisional ball made up to the point where your original ball went and add a penalty stroke and play out the hole with the provisional ball.

If your provisional ball happened to go past the point where your original ball went, don't play your provisional ball until you locate or searched for your original ball for 3 minutes. If you find your ball you must play it and pick up your provisional ball.

Effective 2019, under a new Local Rule, a golf course Committee can elect to give a player an option for dropping a ball without having to go back to the point where you hit the ball that became lost or went OB and when you haven't played a provisional ball.

The Committee has the option to adopt a local rule allowing you to drop another ball and take a two-stroke penalty to speed up play. This local rule helps a player (and pace of play) who hasn't played a provisional ball from going back to the location of the previous stroke. Under this option, you drop your ball in a large relief area which is between two lines.

The first line is established using the "ball reference point" which is a line drawn from the hole to the ball reference point which is the point where the ball was lost or went out of bounds.

The second line is a line drawn from the hole to the "fairway reference point" and the fairway reference point is a point you mark on the nearest edge of the fairway no nearer the hole.

The relief area is between those two lines. Or in other words, in the area between where the ball was lost or went out of bounds and the nearest edge of the fairway (no nearer the hole).

Also, this relief area is extended by two club-lengths on the outside edges of the "ball reference point" and the "fairway reference point" (no nearer the hole).

This local rule is not intended for professional play or high amateur competitions but intended to help speed up the pace of play.

The player is also not allowed to use this option when he has played a provisional ball.

Effective 2019, there is a Model Local Rule for a golf course Committee to adopt which can be found here > USGA, Draft of Model Local Rule, see this link, "Stroke and Distance: Download the draft text as a PDF", and the link is > http://www.usga.org/content/usga/home-page/ruleshub/rules-modernization/major-changes/golfs-new-rulesstroke-and-distance.html

The player is not allowed to use this option when his ball is known to be in a penalty area. If the player's ball is in a penalty area, see the Penalty Area Section of this book on page 51 if your ball went into a penalty area which has its own rules.

OB MARKERS OBSTRUCT YOUR STROKE, STANCE OR SWING – No relief. If you find your ball, and your stroke, stance or swing is obstructed by an OB marker, there is no free relief. You cannot move the OB marker and if you move it, you incur a general penalty (Rule 8 and Definitions).

You can take free relief from artificial objects like a cart path, a building, or a stake marking a penalty area - but not OB markers.

Your options when you are obstructed by an OB marker are: 1) Play the ball as it lies, 2) Take stroke and distance relief by playing again from the spot of your last stroke, or 3) Declare your ball is unplayable and use the unplayable options in the next paragraph (Rule 19).

DECLARING YOUR BALL UNPLAYABLE – Gives you three options, 1. Take stroke and distance relief, 2. Back-on-the-line relief or 3. Take a 2-club length lateral drop no nearer the hole. If you decide your ball is unplayable you take a 1 stroke penalty and you have 3 options: 1) Go back and replay the shot, 2) Take back-on-the-line relief, i. e., go back on the line to a more favorable spot and drop one club-length on either side of the line no nearer the hole, or 3) Stay where you are and drop within two club-lengths no nearer the hole from your ball's present location (Rule 19).

LOOK FOR DESIGNATED DROP ZONES.
Remember to look for designated drop zones for relief.

PENALTY AREAS

COMMITTEE MAY DESIGNATE PENALTY AREAS. There may be areas on a golf course where players frequently lose balls and slow up the pace of play searching for a ball. Effective 2019, a Committee may designate any area(s) as "penalty area(s)".

To keep a good pace of play, a Committee might want to designate high-grassed areas, heavy vegetation areas, and other areas besides lakes, ponds, rivers, ravines, etc., where it is usually difficult to find your ball or play your ball from as "penalty areas." A player can play his ball as it lies in a penalty area or take penalty area relief where he is able to play his ball outside the penalty area (Rule 17).

YELLOW AND RED PENALTY AREAS – Player may play the ball as it lies without penalty. There are two types of penalty areas - Red staked or lined and yellow staked or lined. You can play your ball as it lies (and remove loose impediments, take practice swings, ground your club) in either penalty area but if you decide otherwise, you must take the appropriate penalty area relief for that area (Rule 17).

YELLOW STAKED PENALTY AREA RELIEF – Take stroke and distance relief or back-on-the-line relief. If your ball comes to rest in a yellow staked or lined penalty area, or you are virtually certain it is in a yellow staked penalty area, you can play the ball as it lies, ground your club, remove loose impediments, and take practice swings hitting the ground (Rule 17).

Or, you can take 1 penalty stroke and either 1) Go back to where you hit your previous shot outside the penalty area and take a 1 club-length drop (i.e. take stroke and distance relief), or 2) Take back-on-the-line relief (i.e., go back as far as you like on an extension of a line from the hole to where the ball entered the penalty area) with a 1 club-length drop from the line no nearer the hole (Rule 17).

**RED STAKED PENALTY AREA RELIEF –
Take stroke and distance, back-on-the-line
relief (same as a yellow penalty area) or (in
addition) take a 2 club-length lateral drop**.
If your ball is in or you are virtually certain it is
in a red staked or red-lined penalty area, you
can play the ball as it lies, ground your club,
remove loose impediments, and take practice
swings hitting the ground (Rule 17).

Or, you can take the same two options for relief
as a yellow staked penalty area and in addition
take a 2 club-length lateral drop from the point
where the ball last crossed the edge of the red
penalty area no nearer the hole (Rule 17).

**OK TO GROUND CLUB, TAKE PRACTICE
SWINGS, ETC. IN A PENALTY AREA – Now
allowed**. Prior to 2019, if you were in a hazard
area you incurred a general penalty if you
touched the ground, or grounded your club, or
removed loose impediments. Effective 2019,
you can ground your club behind the ball, take
practice swings, etc. even when your ball is in
water (Rule 17).

REMOVING LOOSE IMPEDIMENTS IN PENALTY AREAS - Allowed. Keep in mind, if you move your ball while removing a loose impediment, you incur a 1 stroke penalty and you must replace your ball to its original position before you moved it. If you decide to play the ball as it lies, you, of course, can't improve the conditions of your shot (e.g., break branches, etc.) or you will incur a general penalty (Rule 17).

NO FREE RELIEF IN A PENALTY AREA FOR ABNORMAL COURSE CONDITIONS OR EMBEDDEDBALL – Player must take penalty area relief. When your ball is in a penalty area, there is no free relief based on abnormal course conditions (e.g., animal hole, ground under repair, immovable obstruction, or temporary water). There's also no embedded ball relief (Rule 17).

NO DECLARING BALL UNPLAYABLE IN A PENALTY AREA – A player must take the appropriate penalty area relief. Penalty areas do not allow you to declare your ball unplayable and use the unplayable options for relief. You, of course, can decide to play the ball as it lies without penalty.

LOST BALL IN PENALTY AREA – If a player is certain his ball went into a penalty area and can't find it, must take the applicable penalty area relief. A ball is deemed lost if not found in 3 minutes and the player must take the appropriate penalty area relief (Rule 17.1c). If the player is not certain his ball went into the penalty area, and cannot find it, he must take stroke and distance relief for a lost ball (Rule 18.2).

NO PLAY ZONE IN A PENALTY AREA – A player must take applicable red or yellow penalty area relief. A player cannot play a ball as it lies in a no play zone and must take penalty relief for a red area or a yellow area as the case might be (Rule 17).

IF BALL IS PARTIALLY ON A PENALTY AREA LINE – It's in the penalty area. A ball is always treated as lying in only one area of the course. If part of the ball touches the edge of a penalty area so that it is say partially in the "general area" and partially in the "penalty area" it is treated as being in the more specific area which would be the penalty area. If a ball comes to rest being partially in two "specific areas," it is treated as lying in the specific area that comes first in this order: 1) penalty area, 2) bunker, 3) putting green (Rule 2 and 17). Since penalty area is the first in this order, the ball is deemed to be in the penalty area.

WATER HAZARDS ARE NOW INCLUDED IN "PENALTY AREAS." Prior to 2019, the old rules referred to "water hazards" which might not have enabled you to take a lateral drop. Bodies of water are now referred to as penalty areas. If the water is marked as a red penalty area, you take red penalty area relief and red marked areas allows 2-club length lateral relief. If the water is marked as a yellow penalty area, you take yellow penalty area relief (stroke and distance relief or back-on-line-relief).

If the water is not marked red or yellow, it's assumed to be red (Penalty Area definition).

DANGEROUS ANIMAL CONDITION IN A PENALTY AREA – Free relief if nearest point of relief is in the penalty area or incur a 1 stroke penalty if the nearest point of relief is outside penalty area. If your ball is inside the penalty area and there is a dangerous animal condition which interferes with your stroke (e.g. poisonous snakes, alligators, wasp nests, etc.), you can take free relief by finding the nearest point of relief (no nearer the hole) inside the penalty area. The nearest point of relief must be inside the penalty area where the dangerous animal condition no longer exists and take a 1 club-length drop (Rule 16).

If there is no nearest point of relief from the dangerous animal condition inside the penalty area, you are limited to take a 1 stroke penalty and the appropriate red or yellow area relief outside the penalty area (Rule 16).

If your ball is not in a penalty area, you can take free relief to the nearest point of relief if you have a dangerous animal condition (Rule 16).

NO OPPOSITE SIDE RELIEF FOR RED PENALTY AREAS. The option to take relief on the opposite margin of a red penalty area is still available by Local Rule. Under the new rule, however, there is no longer an option for a player to take relief on the opposite side of the penalty area (Rule17.1d).

LOST BALL IN PENALTY AREA – 2 scenarios. If you searched for your ball for 3 minutes and can't find it in a penalty area, but you are honestly <u>not</u> certain whether your ball is in the penalty area, you can declare it as a lost ball and take stroke and distance relief (Rule 17).

The second scenario is if you know (or are virtually certain) your ball is in a penalty area but cannot find it, you take penalty area relief in accordance with the appropriate red or yellow staked penalty relief options (Rule 17).

ADVICE (GIVING OR ASKING) IN A PENALTY AREA – Only public information is allowed. You can ask for distances to the green, bunkers, etc. as well as the line of play when you play from a penalty area. You cannot ask for or give advice on what club to play, what swing to make, or ask what is wrong with your swing, etc. (Rule 10).

BALL REMAINS IN PENALTY AREA AFTER STROKE - Procedures. If your ball is in the penalty area after you try to hit out, you take appropriate penalty area relief again plus you can take an additional penalty stroke and go back to where you last made a stroke from outside the penalty area (Rule 17.2a(2)).

BUNKERS

TESTING SAND – A player who deliberately tests the sand incurs a general penalty. If a player deliberately touches the sand to test it, or grounds the club in front or behind the ball or brushes the sand during a practice swing or a backswing, or deliberately touches the sand with an object, the player incurs a general penalty (Rule 12).

ACCIDENTALLY TOUCHING THE SAND – No penalty. Effective 2019, there is no penalty if you happen to touch the sand accidentally with your hand or an object in areas other than the area where you ground your club in front or behind the ball or brush the sand during a practice swing or your backswing. If you are not in these areas, there is no penalty if you don't gain any advantage from it (Rule 12).

LOOSE IMPEDIMENTS CAN BE REMOVED IN BUNKERS. You can remove loose impediments (e.g. stones, twigs, etc.) without penalty and you can reasonably touch the sand while doing so. If you move the ball while removing a loose impediment there is a 1 stroke penalty and you must replace your ball (Rule 15).

PENINSULAS OR ISLANDS OF GRASS, ETC. IN A BUNKER ARE IN THE GENERAL AREA. If your ball comes to rest on an island of grass, weeds, rock, slate, etc. and such which are within the perimeter of the bunker, these islands, etc. are part of the general area and general area rules apply to these areas which allow you to ground your club, take relief for an embedded ball, etc. (Definitions).

REMOVE MOVEABLE OBSTRUCTIONS IN A BUNKER (E.G. THE RAKE) WITHOUT PENALTY. You can remove moveable obstructions without penalty (e.g., the rake, small and large debris, etc.). If your ball moves, you replace your ball to where it was without penalty (Rule 15). If your ball comes to rest on a moveable obstruction (e.g., a towel, paper bag, etc.), drop your ball within 1 club-length in the bunker no nearer the hole (Rule 15).

ABNORMAL COURSE CONDITIONS IN A BUNKER – Free relief if you take a drop in the bunker.   There is free relief in a bunker for interference from 1) an animal hole, 2) ground under repair (G.U.R), 3) immovable obstructions, or 4) temporary water in a bunker and free relief is available in the bunker if these abnormal course conditions interfere with your stance or swing. Find the nearest point of relief in the bunker and drop within one club-length. If you have abnormal course conditions in a bunker, you also have the option to take 1 penalty stroke and drop a ball outside the bunker by going back-on-the-line as far as you want and take a one club-length drop.

If the bunker is full of water and you find your ball, you must take a penalty stroke and back-on-the-line relief outside the bunker (Rule 16).

If the bunker is full of water and you don't find your ball within 3 minutes, it is a lost ball and you must go back to where you last hit it and replay the shot with 1 penalty stroke. You can reasonably search for your ball in the bunker such as raking the water searching for it without penalty (Rule 7).

BALL UNPLAYABLE IN A BUNKER – 4 options for relief. If you decide to declare your ball unplayable in a bunker, there are four options: 1) Take stroke and distance relief with 1 penalty stroke (i.e., go back to where you played your last shot), 2) Take back-on-the-line relief and drop in the bunker with 1 penalty stroke, 3) Take a 2 club-length lateral drop in the bunker with 1 penalty stroke, or 4) take back-on-the-line relief outside the bunker and drop within 1 club length and take 2 penalty strokes (Rule 19).

A PLAYER CAN PLACE CLUBS IN AND RAKE OTHER PARTS OF A BUNKER. You can place a club or equipment in the bunker or rake the bunker in caring for the course without penalty. But you cannot use them to improve any condition which would improve your bunker stroke, your lie, the area of your intended swing or the line of play when you put your equipment in the bunker (e.g., using a club to help you align your shot, etc.). You can rake the bunker after you hit the ball out of the bunker (Rule 12).

IDENTIFYING YOUR BALL IN A BUNKER – Mark and lift it to identify it but clean it only enough to identify it and then recreate the original lie. You may only clean your ball enough to identify it. After you identify it, you put it back in the same lie which means you recreate the original lie, but you may leave a part of the ball visible if it had been covered with sand (Rule 7.1 b and 14).

UNRAKED BUNKER – Must play it as it lies. If a bunker is unraked, full of footprints, etc. which affect your stroke, you must play your ball as it lies and cannot improve your shot or incur a general penalty (Rules 8 and 12).

ANOTHER BALL INTERFERES WITH YOUR STROKE IN THE BUNKER – Ask the other

player to mark his ball. If a player reasonably believes that another player's ball in the bunker might interfere with the player's own play, the player may require the other player to mark the spot and lift the ball. The other player should mark his ball and lift it (but it can't be cleaned). After the first player hits completely out of the bunker, the other player can rake the bunker. The other player then replaces his ball in the same lie (recreates it) as best as he can (Rules 12, 14 and 15).

EMBEDDED BALL IN A BUNKER – You must play it as it lies. If your ball is embedded in a bunker, the ball must be played as it lies. Make sure you identify it since if you play the wrong ball, you incur 2-penalty strokes and then must play your own ball (Rule 12).

IF THE PLAYER'S BALL ROLLS BACK IN THE SAME BUNKER – The player can't rake the bunker to improve his next bunker shot. If your ball remains in the bunker or rolls back into the bunker after you tried to hit it out, you cannot rake the bunker to improve any condition which would improve your next bunker stroke, your lie, the area of your intended swing or the line of play (Rule 12).

PLAYER HITS OUT OF A BUNKER AND HIS BALL GOES OB OR IS LOST – Player may rake the bunker before playing his next shot. Once you hit out of a bunker, you can rake it. If your ball went OB or is lost and you are taking stroke and distance relief, rake the bunker before replaying the shot. Take a drop in the bunker within one club-length from where you hit the ball OB or became lost (Rules 12, 14 and 18).

LOST BALL IN BUNKER – Must take stroke and distance relief. If you search for your ball in a bunker and can't find it in 3 minutes, it is a lost ball and you must take stroke and distance relief and go back to the point where you played your last shot. You are permitted to rake the bunker to search for your ball and replace the ball if you move it while searching for it in the bunker (Rule 7).

DANGEROUS ANIMAL CONDITION IN A BUNKER – Free relief if nearest point of relief is in the bunker, otherwise, the player incurs 1 penalty stroke if the nearest point of relief is outside the bunker. You can take free relief to the nearest point of relief if you encounter a dangerous animal condition in a bunker (Rule 12). If a dangerous animal condition interferes with your stroke or stance (e.g. poisonous snakes, wasp nests, alligators, fire ants, etc.), you can take free relief by finding the nearest point of relief (no nearer the hole) inside the bunker. The nearest point of relief must be inside the bunker area where the dangerous animal condition no longer exists and take a 1 club-length drop (Rule 16).

If there is no nearest point of relief from the dangerous animal condition inside the bunker, you must take a 1 stroke penalty and back-on-the-line relief outside the bunker (Rules 12 and 16).

GREENS

BALL COMES TO REST ON WRONG GREEN – Take a free drop off the green so your stance and intended swing will not encounter the green. Previously, if your ball came to rest on the wrong green you had to play your ball from the nearest point of relief off the green no closer to the hole and you could take your stance on the green itself to play your next shot. Effective 2019, you are not allowed to take your stance on the green or to take a stance where the path of your swing might encounter the surface of the green so drop your ball accordingly no nearer the hole (Rule 13).

SPRINKLER HEADS, DRAINS, ETC. – Free relief if your ball lies on the sprinkler head (or another immovable obstruction) if the obstruction interferes with your stance or swing. You can take free relief if your ball is in the general area and comes to rest on a sprinkler head or drain or if it interferes with your stance or swing. If so, take a drop within 1 club-length no nearer the hole. If you are chipping or putting to get your ball on the green and a sprinkler head, drain, etc. (an immovable obstruction) is in your line of play but not obstructing your stance or swing, you must play your ball as it lies (Rule 16).

A BALL WHICH IS PARTIALLY ON THE GREEN AND PARTIALLY ON THE FRINGE IS TREATED AS BEING ON THE GREEN (A SPECIFIC AREA). If your ball is both on the green and the general area (e.g., it is both on the fringe – which is the general area – and the green), then your ball is on the specific area which is the green (Rule 2).

MARK YOUR BALL ON THE GREEN AND AVOID PLAYING IT FROM THE WRONG PLACE. As you walk on the green look for your ball mark and repair it. Mark your ball with a ball marker and if your ball might be in another players line, move the marker a putter head away and remember to move it back before you hit your putt. If you don't move it back, you will play the ball from the wrong spot and incur a general penalty (Rule 14).

PLAYING WRONG BALL – If you discover on the green you played the wrong ball you must locate your ball and go back and play it. In stroke play, there is a 2-stroke penalty if you played the wrong ball. After taking the 2-stroke penalty, assess the situation and go back and locate and play your own ball. If your own ball is lost, you treat it as a lost ball and go back to where you hit it before it became lost.

If it turns out another player is playing your ball, the other player must likewise go back and correct the mistake and take a 2-stroke penalty for hitting the wrong ball.

The stroke made with the wrong ball (and any more strokes) does not count. If you don't correct the mistake before making a stroke to begin the next hole you are disqualified.

If you are on the final green, you need to go back and correct it before turning in your scorecard or be disqualified (Rule 6).

In match play, the penalty for playing the wrong ball is loss of hole. If the players hit each other's ball, the first to make a stroke at a wrong ball gets loss of hole. If it is not known which wrong ball was played first, there is no penalty and the hole must be played out with the balls exchanged (Rule 6).

PUTTING ORDER – Furthers from the hole goes first. In stroke play, there is no penalty for putting out of order unless it gives another player an advantage (e.g., if a player intentionally plays out of turn to give another player the line of a putt). If this occurs, the two players each incur a general penalty (Rule 6).

In match play, if your opponent putts out of order you can cancel the stroke and require him to replay the putt (Rule 6).

The players can also agree to play out of turn to save time in match play or agree to play ready golf in stroke play (Rule 5).

PUTTING WITH THE FLAGSTICK IN - Allowed.
Effective 2019, there is no longer any penalty if you hit the flagstick with your putt. You have the option of leaving the flagstick in for a putt without incurring a penalty (Rule 13).

PLAYER ACCIDENTALLY MOVES BALL OR BALL MARKER – No penalty.
There is no penalty if you, an opponent or another player accidentally move your ball or ball-marker on the putting green (Rule 13). You must replace your ball to where it was. In match play, if your opponent deliberately touches or causes your ball to move, he incurs a 1 stroke penalty (Rule 9).

USING A CLUB TO ALLIGN A PUTT – Not allowed.
Previously, a player could lay a club down on the green and use the shaft of the club to help align the putt. Effective 2019, that is no

longer allowed on the green or else you incur a general penalty (Rule 10).

PLAYER'S BALL IS MOVED BY ANOTHER BALL – Replace it without penalty. If your ball is on the green and is moved by another ball you must replace it without penalty. If the exact spot is unknown, you best estimate the spot and replace your ball on that spot (Rule 9). In stroke play, if your opponent *intentionally* moves your ball, he incurs a 1 stroke penalty and you must replace your ball. If it was accidental, there is no penalty (Rule 9).

ABNORMAL COURSE CONDITIONS ON GREEN – Free relief. If you are on the green and an abnormal course condition interferes with your line of play (e.g., G.U.R., temporary water, etc.) you can take free relief by placing the ball at the nearest point of relief which can be on the green or general area (e.g., the fringe) no nearer the hole. You place the ball (don't drop it) on the nearest point of relief (Rule 16).

REMOVE LOOSE IMPEDIMENTS, MOVEABLE OBSTRUCTIONS, SAND, AND LOOSE SOIL ON THE GREEN – No penalty if ball moves. Loose impediments like leaves, etc. as well as sand and loose soil can be removed on the putting green. If you accidentally move your ball marker or ball when doing this, you replace your ball to where it was without penalty (Rule 13).

REPAIRING SPIKE MARKS AND OTHER DAMAGE ON THE GREEN - Allowed.
Effective 2019, you now can reasonably repair almost any damage, i.e., spike marks, pitch marks, etc. anywhere on the green including the hole if it is damaged – but not natural wear.

Keep in mind you can reasonably repair "damage" and you can't improve the line of your putt to the hole beyond repairing damage. That means you can't go overboard improving the line of play of your putt or you incur a general penalty.

You also cannot improve any natural imperfections. For example, aeration holes, natural surface imperfections or natural wearing down are not considered damage but natural surface imperfections (Rule 13).

OK TO TOUCH THE LINE OF YOUR PUTT ON THE GREEN. Previously, you or your caddy were not allowed to touch your line of play on the green or you incur a 1 stroke penalty. Effective 2019, you or your caddy can touch the line (Rule 10 and 13).

BALL MOVES WHEN A PLAYER MARKS OR WHEN A PLAYER TAKES AWAY MARKER – No penalty and player must replace his ball to where it was. If your ball moves accidentally when you place or take away your ball marker or moves when you accidentally brush with your foot or club, there is no penalty, but you must replace it to where it was (if you don't replace it you incur a general penalty).

If your ball simply moves *before* you mark it, you must play your ball as it lies from the spot it moved to.

Effective 2019, if you have marked your ball and then replace it on the green and it moves by itself, you must replace it to its original position without penalty (Rules 9 and 13).

EMBEDDED BALL – Free relief. If your ball is embedded on the putting green, mark the spot and lift and clean the ball, repair the damage caused by the ball's impact, and replace the ball on its original spot (Rule 13).

TEMPORARY WATER ON THE GREEN – Free relief. You can take free relief from temporary water on the green since it's an abnormal course condition (Rule 16). Take free relief at the nearest point of relief no nearer the hole by placing it down on the spot and letting it go. If the ball should roll away, replace it again. If it rolls away a second time, place your ball at the nearest point (no closer to the hole) where it doesn't roll away (Rule 14).

ADVICE ABOUT THE LINE OF PLAY ON THE GREEN – Not allowed. In the other areas of the course, you can ask about the line of play (e.g., you can ask for the line of play if you are in a very deep greenside bunker, ravine, etc.). You are not allowed to ask or give advice to another player how a putt will break, or you will incur a general penalty. You can ask or give advice to your playing partner (Rule 10).

CAN'T TEST GREEN DURING PLAY. You are not allowed to roll a ball on or rub the grass on the green you are about to play, or you incur a general penalty. Between holes you may do this on the green just played or on a practice green (Rule 13).

PLAYER NOT ALLOWED TO ANCHOR PUTTER AGAINST HIS BODY. You're not allowed to anchor your putter or any club directly to your body or indirectly to your body such as holding a forearm against your body during a stroke or you incur a general penalty. The handle of the putter resting against your forearm is not considered to be anchoring the putter against your body if your forearm isn't anchored to your body (Rule 10).

A PUTT HITS ANOTHER BALL ON THE GREEN: PLAYER WHO HITS ANOTHER BALL AT REST ON THE GREEN WHILE PUTTING – Incurs a 2-shot penalty in stroke play. In stroke play, if you are on the green and your putt hits another ball at rest on the green, you incur a 2-stroke penalty. The ball that was hit must be put back to where it was (Rule 11).

PLAYER HITS FLAGSTICK OR PERSON TENDING IT – Play it as it lies without penalty. There is no penalty for hitting the pin or accidentally hitting the person tending it and you play the ball where it comes to rest (Rule 11 and 13).

If a club or other object (like the flagstick) is intentionally laid down on the green to stop the ball and you hit it with your putt, you incur a general penalty and the putt must be replayed (Rule 11).

A BALL RESTING AGAINST THE FLAGSTICK AND PART OF THE BALL IS BELOW THE SURFACE IS CONSIDERED HOLED OUT. Except when ball is embedded in the side of the hole. If a player's ball comes to rest against the flagstick left in the hole then if any part of the ball is below the surface of the putting green, the ball is treated as holed out even if the entire ball is not below the surface (Rule 13). If a ball is embedded in the side of the hole it may not be considered to be holed out unless the whole of the ball is below the surface since the words "resting against the flagstick" imply the ball that is free to move so it would fall into the hole if the flagstick wasn't there. An embedded ball wouldn't be resting against the flagstick.

A BALL OVERHANGS THE HOLE – Maximum waiting time for ball dropping in is a reasonable approach time plus 10 seconds. The player is allowed a reasonable time to reach the hole plus ten more seconds to wait to see whether the ball which overhangs the hole will fall into the hole (Rule 13).

If your ball does not fall into the hole during this waiting time, your ball is treated as being at rest. But if your ball then falls into the hole after this time limit has passed and before it is played, you have holed out with the previous stroke, but you get one penalty stroke added to your score for the hole (Rule 13).

CONCEDING PUTTS – OK in match play but not in stroke play. You can concede a putt (or any shot) in match play by telling your opponent to pick up. Conceding a putt in stroke play is not allowed and you must hole-out. If a player picks up, he incurs 1 penalty stroke. Also, he must replace his ball and hole out or be DQd (Rules 3 and 9).

LOOSING A CLUB – You must play without it unless it's found. Players sometimes leave a club around a green and go on to the next hole. If you recover it later, you can use it, but if not, you can't add another club to your bag or borrow a club. You must play without it (Rule 4).

We'd love to hear from you!

Image: Creative Commons

"There usually is a way to do things better and Edison there is opportunity when you find it." - Thomas Edison

If you have a question on a rule or a different opinion on a rule, please let us know and email us your thoughts. Our email is TeamGolfwell@gmail.com.

About the Authors

TeamGolfwell are bestselling authors. Their books have sold thousands of copies including several #1 bestsellers in golf and sports humor.

Contact us at TeamGolfwell@gmail.com for anything. We love to hear from our fans!

www.TeamGolfwell.com

Thank you very much for your interest in our book and we hope you enjoyed our book and it helps you.

If you liked our book, we would appreciate your leaving a very brief review on Amazon and/or Goodreads if you have the time. Thank you and happy golfing!

Sincerely,

The TeamGolfwell

Made in the USA
Coppell, TX
06 December 2020